I0023514

The Influence of Psychological Trauma in Nursing

STUDENT WORKBOOK

Karen J. Foli, PhD, RN, FAAN

John R. Thompson, MD

Sigma
GLOBAL NURSING
EXCELLENCE

The Sigma Theta Tau International Honor Society of Nursing (Sigma) is a nonprofit organization whose mission is advancing world health and celebrating nursing excellence in scholarship, leadership, and service. Founded in 1922, Sigma has more than 135,000 active members in over 90 countries and territories. Members include practicing nurses, instructors, researchers, policymakers, entrepreneurs, and others. Sigma's more than 530 chapters are located at more than 700 institutions of higher education throughout Armenia, Australia, Botswana, Brazil, Canada, Colombia, England, Ghana, Hong Kong, Ireland, Japan, Jordan, Kenya, Lebanon, Malawi, Mexico, the Netherlands, Nigeria, Pakistan, Philippines, Portugal, Puerto Rico, Singapore, South Africa, South Korea, Swaziland, Sweden, Taiwan, Tanzania, Thailand, the United States, and Wales. Learn more at www.sigmanursing.org.

Sigma Theta Tau International
550 West North Street
Indianapolis, IN, USA 46202

To order additional books, buy in bulk, or order for corporate use, contact Sigma Marketplace at 888.654.4968 (US and Canada) or +1.317.634.8171 (outside US and Canada).

To request a review copy for course adoption, email solutions@sigmamarketplace.org or call 888.654.4968 (US and Canada) or +1.317.634.8171 (outside US and Canada).

To request author information, or for speaker or other media requests, contact Sigma Marketing at 888.634.7575 (US and Canada) or +1.317.634.8171 (outside US and Canada).

ISBN: 9781948057076

First Printing, 2019

Publisher: Dustin Sullivan
Acquisitions Editor: Emily Hatch
Cover Designer: Rebecca Batchelor
Interior Design/Page Layout: Rebecca Batchelor
Managing Editor: Carla Hall
Development and Project Editor: Rebecca Senninger
Copy Editor: Gill Editorial Services
Proofreader: Todd Lothery

DEDICATION

This student workbook is dedicated to nurses who seek healing
from trauma within themselves and who seek
healing for others.

ACKNOWLEDGMENTS

The goal of any work is to ensure that the aim and audience are always kept in the center of the authors' efforts. Our aim—to increase insight into personal trauma and build trauma awareness and resilience in new nurses—was always in the forefront of our energies. As we sought to secure a home for this book, we believed this book was needed and would ultimately improve the quality of nurses' lives and enhance patient-centered care.

We are grateful to Sigma and its publishing staff. To Emily Hatch, thank you for our first meeting during which you advised Karen to think more broadly in nursing education, while focusing the work. To Carla Hall, for encouragement, great communication throughout the process, and assisting with book graphics and permissions. To Dustin Sullivan, who supported and celebrated with us as we completed this book. And finally, to the Sigma publishing committee, who requested companion books so that students could apply trauma-informed nursing care through simulations. In summary, thank you for believing in this book.

Specific to the instructor's guide and student workbook, we extend a special acknowledgment to the National League for Nursing for allowing us to adapt its Simulation Design Template, which was originally adapted from the work of Childs, Sepples, and Chambers (2007). We greatly appreciate their generosity in allowing us to use this intellectual property.

ABOUT THE AUTHORS

Karen J. Foli, PhD, RN, FAAN, received her associate's and bachelor's degrees from Indiana State University and her master's degree, with an emphasis in nursing administration, from Indiana University School of Nursing, Indianapolis. Dr. Foli received her PhD in communications from the University of Illinois, Urbana–Champaign. She is an Associate Professor and the Director of the PhD in Nursing Program at Purdue University School of Nursing, West Lafayette, Indiana.

Foli is a fellow in the American Academy of Nursing (AAN) in recognition for her work with nontraditional families, such as adoption and kinship families. She is a member of the Child, Adolescent, and Family Expert Panel through the AAN. She has forwarded a mid-range theory of parental postadoption depression and has tested this theory in empirical studies. Her research is bound together to alleviate the suffering of psychological trauma. She is currently examining the role of psychological trauma in substance use in registered nurses.

A recipient of numerous teaching awards, including the Charles B. Murphy Outstanding Undergraduate Teaching Award from Purdue University, the highest award bestowed for undergraduate teaching at the university, Foli takes pride in being a nurse educator. In 2018, she was one of 45 faculty members who were inducted into the Purdue University Book of Great Teachers, signifying excellence in teaching. She also received the Sigma Theta Tau International Honor Society of Nursing Delta Omicron Chapter Award for Outstanding Mentoring in 2017. Preparing nurse scientists is also an important part of Foli's professional work. As the director of the PhD in Nursing Program, she encourages and guides students and faculty in preparing nurses who will continue to explore and build upon the science of nursing.

Foli's lifelong love of writing has produced works in a wide range of formats and genres, including memoir, regulatory writing in the pharmaceutical industry, scholarly writing of empirical studies, and mystery short stories. She is author or coauthor of four well-received health-related books. One of these, *Nursing Care of Adoption and Kinship Families: A Clinical Guide for Advanced Practice Nurses* (2017, Springer), received the American Psychiatric Nurses Association (APNA) Award for Media in 2018. This award "recognizes APNA members who have demonstrated excellence in producing media related to psychiatric-mental health nursing."

A special passion of Foli's work is advancing the conceptualization of nursing and the "work" of nurses. The elusive definition of nursing motivates her efforts to forward a way to value and communicate what nurses do in practice, in education, in policy, and in research. She has partnered with many graduate students and coauthored several papers that define important concepts surrounding nursing care.

Her appreciation for nurses and the profession of nursing is unique in that her career path veered away from the profession for a time and carried her into professional writing, teaching business communications in a Big Ten business school, and writing global experimental research protocols for a large pharmaceutical company. When she returned to the world of nursing, Foli realized how much society needs the special comfort, caring, and compassion offered by nurses. Her deep appreciation for what nurses experience motivated her to write this book to prepare students and those new to the field to become stronger and more resilient as they process and encounter patients in crises and in need of trauma-informed care.

———————

Foli and her coauthor, John R. Thompson, have been married for almost three decades and have three adult children. Avid dog lovers, they have always been owners of at least three dogs, many times taking in strays and "dumped" animals who became loved members of their family.

John R. Thompson, MD, has practiced as a physician in the specialty area of psychiatry for the past 30 years. He completed his residency in general psychiatry and a fellowship in child/adolescent psychiatry in the Department of Psychiatry at Indiana University. Since Thompson's fellowship, he has worked with a variety of populations, including children, adolescents, young adults, and adults, including addiction psychiatry. He has practiced in multiple healthcare contexts: acute care/inpatient care, intensive outpatient, community mental health, consult-liaison, veterans' mental health, and forensic psychiatry. Along with Karen Foli, he is coauthor of *The Post-Adoption Blues: Overcoming the Unforeseen Challenges of Adoption* (Rodale, 2004).

Currently, he practices psychiatric medicine for Purdue University's Counseling and Psychological Services, West Lafayette, Indiana. In this position, Thompson evaluates and manages the psychiatric needs of students enrolled in higher education. Common issues include depression, anxiety, substance use, personality disorders, attention deficit disorder, and healing from trauma.

Thompson is also a cancer survivor; thus, his insights into trauma are both personal and professional. In his medical practice, he assesses and counsels young adults who are processing and recovering from trauma. Thompson approaches the individual in a trauma-informed, holistic way. He strives to promote a feeling of safety and allows the individual to share past experiences as the relationship is built and trust evolves. He believes in "de-prescribing" medications—removing those agents that create addictions, lack a therapeutic rationale, or are interacting with other agents in nontherapeutic ways. Taking time to review medical records, Thompson pieces together past traumas, dual diagnoses, and concurrent medical conditions that, when revealed, contribute to optimal care. Recognizing that healthcare disparities and social determinants of health result in individuals struggling to secure resources in filling prescriptions and in the wider community, he searches for affordable healthcare and orders appropriate referrals to provide for a continuum of care.

Growing up in the Rocky Mountains of Colorado, Thompson enjoys nature and being outdoors. His spirit is recharged upon seeing growth both in his plants and trees, and more importantly, in people. Being part of students' success, seeing them achieve their career goals as they develop as young adults, motivates Thompson to continue to offer each individual his best efforts as a medical provider.

THE INFLUENCE OF PSYCHOLOGICAL TRAUMA IN NURSING

STUDENT WORKBOOK

TABLE OF CONTENTS

INTRODUCTION

By now as a student nurse, you may have participated in simulation activities. This instructional method is designed to provide rich learning experiences to complement clinical activities with "real patients." Simulation situates the student in a safe environment where mistakes can be made without the risk of patient injury. When discussing the care offered to those who have experienced a traumatic event, minimizing risk to patients and maximizing safety are paramount. In the following simulations, you—the student and soon to be licensed nurse—may be the focus of care. This is a shift in thinking for many nurses because we often ignore our needs and emotional reactions to the intense stimuli of what we see, hear, touch, and experience at the bedside. In the same way, kindness and compassion toward your peers and the individuals who assume roles taken in the activities are essential and integrated into the simulations. These behaviors are intricately linked to trauma-informed care, the major theme of this workbook and simulations. This student workbook is designed as a companion to the primary book, *The Influence of Psychological Trauma in Nursing,* which digs deep into psychological trauma in nurses and nursing care, as well as approaches to healing.

PURPOSE AND STRUCTURE

The purpose of *The Influence of Psychological Trauma in Nursing: Student Workbook* is to provide content for simulation experiences related to psychological trauma. The simulations are based on composite cases; therefore, they do not represent any specific individual. Still, you may be inclined to identify with the individuals in the simulations or be reminded of someone you know in these scenarios. In Figure 1.1, we conceptualize trauma from both individual and nurse-specific perspectives. The six simulations concentrate on those events that student nurses and those new to the profession are most likely to encounter. Three sections divide the workbook temporally and by role: the student nurse during college (student and peers), the student during college (student as new caregiver), and after graduation (new nurse in the workforce). Specifically, the six simulations address the trauma of bullying (centered around sexual minority status), posttraumatic stress disorder (PTSD; veteran experiencing posttraumatic stress symptoms), second-victim trauma (student nurse who makes a medication error), secondary traumatic stress (student nurse witnesses unexpected death), system-induced trauma (patient who is agitated and nonadherent), and workplace violence (new nurse who has been injured by patient). Many of these types of trauma can be located on the right side of the trauma circle in Figure 1.1.

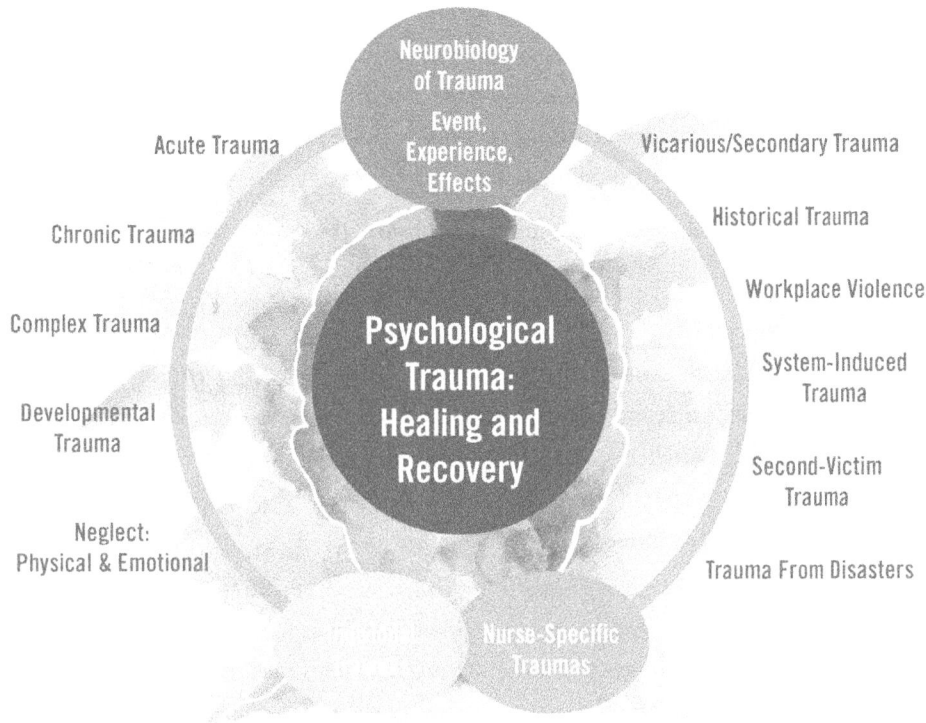

FIGURE 1.1 Conceptualizing trauma.

Our hope is that the student workbook will aid in preparing you as a student and as a newly licensed nurse and support you as you build resiliency. We also hope that these simulations inform you at a personal level about the often-overlooked influences of psychological trauma in your own life.

PREPARING FOR SIMULATIONS

Let's get to a quick primer on psychological trauma and trauma-informed care. You probably have heard about trauma-level health centers. These centers are equipped and sourced with trained caregivers to render care to those in need of life-saving services. Psychological trauma may accompany physical trauma, and the psychological aspect of trauma is the focus of these simulations. The Substance Abuse and Mental Health Services Administration (SAMHSA, 2014a, n.p.) refers to psychological trauma as:

> experiences that cause intense physical and psychological stress reactions. It can refer to a single event, multiple events, or a set of circumstances that is experienced by an individual as physically and emotionally harmful or threatening and that has lasting adverse effects on the individual's physical, social, emotional, or spiritual well-being.

Deconstructing this description, we can quickly discern that there is a stress reaction. The individual has both a physiological and an emotional response to the event. Next, in addition to an immediate response to perceived harm or threat, there are effects after the event. These effects vary with individuals but may impact various dimensions of well-being. A trauma-informed nurse understands this definition and knows past trauma influences assessment and management of care.

But what is "trauma-informed care"? We found a definition that is comprehensive and incorporates the goals of being trauma-informed:

> (1) to understand how violence and victimization have figured in the lives of most consumers of mental health, substance abuse, and other services and (2) to apply that understanding in providing services and designing service systems so that they accommodate the needs and vulnerabilities of trauma survivors and facilitate client participation in treatment. (Butler, Critelli, & Rinfrette, 2011, p. 178)

Of note in this definition is that trauma affects "most consumers" (Butler et al., 2011, p. 178). This is of healthcare significance. The occurrence of trauma has been framed as a major contributor to our public health crisis (Shern, Blanch, & Steverman, 2016). When nurses are trauma-informed, they invite individuals to become true partners in managing their health by acknowledging and accommodating what has happened to them in life (SAMHSA-HRSA Center for Integrated Health Solutions, n.d.). We believe caregivers, in turn, are more likely to appreciate patients' perspectives and choices if or when adherence becomes an issue.

Beyond this definition, guiding principles can help you implement trauma-informed care (see Table 1.1; SAMHSA, 2014b). Providing safety—psychological and physical—is the first principle. Without safety, the individual has difficulty attending to messages and is consumed with feeling safe, even at an unconscious level. These simulations may trigger a memory of something in you. It is important to gauge your level of comfort and communicate this to your instructor.

TABLE 1.1   SAMHSA'S SIX GUIDING PRINCIPLES OF TRAUMA-INFORMED CARE

Principle 1: Safety
Principle 2: Trustworthiness and transparency
Principle 3: Peer support and mutual self-help
Principle 4: Collaboration and mutuality
Principle 5: Empowerment, voice, and choice
Principle 6: Cultural, historical, and gender issues

Source: SAMHSA, 2014b

In the second principle, nurses must extend promises they are able to keep and be transparent in these messages—even if such messages convey they don't have the answers to difficult questions. Peer support and mutual self-help apply to nurses as caregivers to self, peers, and patients. Collaborating with others, a healthcare team including mental health professionals is another principle of trauma-informed care. Often in delivering care, we are less apt to offer empowerment, voice, and choices to those around us. The need to be efficient, stay on task, and emphasize the empirical side of nursing often dampens a spirit of empowering those we help. Acknowledging and being sensitive to how culture, gender, generational trauma, and your own histories affect interpretation of traumatic events is the last principle.

Now, the big question that many of you may be thinking is: "OK, how do we prepare for these simulations?" In addition to the videos, training modules, and readings for the specific simulations, there are knowledge and skills to review for each simulation. To prepare for the simulations we've outlined, we recommend the following:

- Review the definitions of trauma (see SAMHSA, 2014a) and trauma-informed care (Butler et al., 2011).

- Map the types of trauma specific to nursing (see Figure 1.1).

- Describe the scenario from a micro (individual) and macro (system) perspective.

- Practice the basic therapeutic communications skills (summarizing, reflecting, exploring, restating, therapeutic silence, and so forth).

- Internalize the six guiding principles of trauma-informed care (see Table 1.1; SAMHSA, 2014b).

The last task to do prior to participating in the simulations is to balance how you know what you know in nursing. Carper (1978) and Chinn and Kramer (2015) list the five ways to describe nurses' knowledge or ways of knowing:

- Empirical: This is the science of nursing: reading lab values, understanding how medications work in the body, and learning how the body heals.

- Ethical: This is the way you navigate right and wrong. It is how you learn from the American Nurses Association's Code of Ethics (2015).

- Esthetic/art of nursing: This knowing allows you to hold a hand when needed or to balance an assignment so that you deliver care mindfully and seamlessly.

- The ability to know the Self: This is the ability to know who you are and to acknowledge that your continued learning is part of your journey.

- Emancipatory: This is the ability to look beyond circumstances and see how social justice and the determinants of health can affect our actions. (Carper, 1978; Chinn & Kramer, 2015)

The temptation—at times—is to emphasize our empirical knowledge. It is important to know the science behind our care: to grasp when lab values are abnormal and to be able to communicate to team members the patient's vital signs, oxygenation level, and wound healing. In psychological trauma, we must understand how our brain and body react to actual harm and threats of harm. Empirical knowledge informs us and is balanced with our other ways of knowing as we offer care to those who have experienced traumatic events. Examples include esthetic knowing as we sit beside an individual, sharing that person's pain through respectful silence; ethical knowing as we avoid retraumatizing a patient through patient-centered care; emancipatory knowing as we view the individual within a society whose perspectives and choices are shaped by social determinants; and finally, knowing ourselves as we look into our mirrors and see ourselves at the bedside, helping others.

CONCLUSION

The following six simulations are reflective of the content of *The Influence of Psychological Trauma in Nursing*. Reading the primary book will enable you to understand the broader descriptions of trauma that influence nurses, both as individuals and as professionals. The primary book will also set the foundation for these simulations. Therefore, the major goals of the following six scenarios are: 1) to prime you for lifelong learning in this area, 2) to explore ways of knowing and trauma-informed care, and 3) to apply these to your life, your peers' lives, and your patients' well-being.

REFERENCES

American Nurses Association. (2015). *Code of ethics for nurses with interpretive statements.* Silver Spring, MD: Author.

Butler, L. D., Critelli, F. M., & Rinfrette, E. S. (2011). Trauma-informed care and mental health. *Directions in Psychiatry, 31,* 197–210.

Carper, B. A. (1978). Fundamental patterns of knowing in nursing. *Advances in Nursing Science, 1*(1), 13–24.

Chinn, P., & Kramer, M. (2015). *Knowledge development in nursing: Theory and process* (9th ed.). St. Louis, MO: Mosby, Inc.

SAMHSA-HRSA Center for Integrated Health Solutions. (n.d.). Trauma. Retrieved from https://www.integration.samhsa.gov/clinical-practice/trauma-informed

Shern, D. L., Blanch, A. K., & Steverman, S. M. (2016). Toxic stress, behavioral health, and the next major era in public health. *American Journal of Orthopsychiatry, 86*(2), 109–123. doi: http://dx.doi.org/10.1037/ort0000120

Substance Abuse and Mental Health Services Administration. (2014a). Key terms: Definitions. *SAMHSA News, 22*(2). Retrieved from https://www.samhsa.gov/samhsaNewsLetter/Volume_22_Number_2/trauma_tip/key_terms.html

Substance Abuse and Mental Health Services Administration. (2014b). *SAMHSA's concept of trauma and guidance for a trauma-informed approach.* HHS Publication No. (SMA) 14-4884. Rockville, MD: Author.

SECTION 1

TRAUMA DURING COLLEGE:
THE STUDENT NURSE AND PEERS

INTERPERSONAL TRAUMA: SEXUAL IDENTITY BULLYING

A transgender individual (male-to-female; MTF), Khris is in her sophomore year of nursing and has been assigned an observation day in the operating room with other student nurses. While changing, two peers observe that Khris still has the anatomy of a biological male. Unknown to her peers, Khris has a history of harassment and bullying from peers, and she attempted suicide (ingestion of mother's benzodiazepine) during her freshman year of high school.

SIMULATION LEARNING OBJECTIVES

1. Employ strategies to reduce risk of harm to peers.

2. Communicate with peers in a manner that illustrates caring, reflects cultural awareness, and addresses psychosocial needs.

3. Demonstrate knowledge of legal and ethical obligations.

SIMULATION SCENARIO OBJECTIVES

1. Reflect on actions taken by self and peers.

2. Apply the principles of trauma-informed care to individuals who identify as sexual minorities.

3. Discuss ways to create safe spaces and acceptance of LGBTQ individuals.

PRIOR TO THE SIMULATION, THE STUDENT SHOULD:

WATCH THE VIDEOS:

- GLSEN. (2017). *How to support transgender students*. Retrieved from https://www.youtube.com/watch?v=kq19QdOfH1Y

- The National Child Traumatic Stress Network. (2015). *Safe places, safe spaces: Creating welcoming and inclusive environments for traumatized LGBTQ youth*. Retrieved from https://www.nctsn.org/resources/safe-places-safe-spaces-creating-welcoming-and-inclusive-environments-traumatized-lgbtq-0

READ:

Aul, K. (2017). Who's uncivil to who? Perceptions of incivility in pre-licensure nursing programs. *Nursing Education in Practice, 27,* 36–44. doi: http://dx.doi.org/10.1016/j.nepr.2017.08.016

El-Azeem Ibrahim, S. A., & Ahmed Qalawa, S. (2016). Factors affecting nursing students' incivility: As perceived by students and faculty staff. *Nurse Education Today, 36,* 118–123. doi: http://dx.doi.org/10.1016/j.nedt.2015.08.014

National Child Traumatic Stress Network, Child Sexual Abuse Collaborative Group. (2014). *LGBTQ youth and sexual abuse: Information for mental health professionals*. Los Angeles, CA, and Durham, NC: National Center for Child Traumatic Stress. Retrieved from https://www.nctsn.org/sites/default/files/resources//lgbtq_youth_sexual_abuse_professionals.pdf

PREBRIEFING/BRIEFING

The objectives of this simulation are to learn about civility and how to mitigate sexual minority stress through trauma-informed communications and actions.

Simulation Design Template (revised March 2018) © 2018, National League for Nursing. Originally adapted from Childs, Sepples, & Chambers (2007), Designing simulations for nursing education. In P. R. Jeffries (Ed.), *Simulation in nursing education: From conceptualization to evaluation* (pp. 42–58). Washington, DC: National League for Nursing.

Link to original template: https://sirc.nln.org/pluginfile.php/18733/mod_page/content/51/Simulation%20Design%20Template%202018.docx

POSTTRAUMATIC STRESS DISORDER: MILITARY VETERAN AND STUDENT

Mark is a 26-year-old army veteran who is enrolled in a two-year community college nursing program. After serving two deployments to Afghanistan where he saw active combat, he returned home one year ago. Due to a diagnosis of posttraumatic stress disorder (PTSD), Mark is in therapy to decrease his symptoms (recurrent nightmares and anxiety) and strengthen his marriage. After speaking with several career counselors, he decided to enroll in nursing school. Mark does not feel part of his student nursing community and is unsure whether entering school was the right decision. He is struggling, feeling he is conspicuous and isolated with little in common with his peers.

SIMULATION LEARNING OBJECTIVES

1. Employ strategies to reduce risk of harm to the peer.

2. Conduct assessments appropriate for the care of the peer in an organized and systematic manner.

3. Communicate with the peer in a manner that illustrates caring, reflects cultural awareness, and addresses psychosocial needs.

4. Make clinical judgments and decisions that are evidence-based.

5. Demonstrate knowledge of legal and ethical obligations.

SIMULATION SCENARIO OBJECTIVES

1. Assess for signs of PTSD within the context of veteran status.

2. Integrate knowledge of PTSD symptoms with trauma-informed assessment and immediate support.

3. Provide physical and psychological safety for the individual who is affected by a trauma trigger.

PRIOR TO THE SIMULATION, THE STUDENT SHOULD:

WATCH THE VIDEO:

- Burke Jr., T. (2015). *PTSD and returning to the classroom.* TEDxYale. Retrieved from https://www.youtube.com/watch?v=XBGNJQWSYHY

READ:

Barry, A. E., Whiteman, S. D., & MacDermid Wadsworth, S. M. (2012). Implications of posttraumatic stress among military-affiliated and civilian students. *Journal of American College Health, 60*(8), 562–573. doi: 10.1080/07448481.2012.721427

PREBRIEFING/BRIEFING

This simulation focuses on the team working during a code blue. One of your peers may not be able to continue with the simulation; in that case, it is acceptable to end the code to render care to your peer. The objectives of this simulation are to become aware of how triggers of past traumatic events may affect individuals and how to respond in a therapeutic manner.

Simulation Design Template (revised March 2018) © 2018, National League for Nursing. Originally adapted from Childs, Sepples, & Chambers (2007), Designing simulations for nursing education. In P. R. Jeffries (Ed.), *Simulation in nursing education: From conceptualization to evaluation* (pp. 42–58). Washington, DC: National League for Nursing.

Link to original template: https://sirc.nln.org/pluginfile.php/18733/mod_page/content/51/Simulation%20Design%20Template%202018.docx

SECTION 2

TRAUMA DURING COLLEGE: THE STUDENT NURSE AS CAREGIVER

SECOND-VICTIM TRAUMA: OVERWHELMED IN MED-SURG

MELANIE SIMULATION

Melanie is a junior in her baccalaureate nursing program and is in the first week of clinical. She needs to prepare and administer medications at 0900. Her first patient is a 67-year-old male with a history of alcohol dependency and atrial fibrillation. He was admitted for an emergency repair of an open femur fracture (open reduction internal fixation of the right distal femur) following a motor vehicular accident. Twelve hours post-operatively, the patient experienced an upper gastrointestinal bleed with hematemesis, confirmed with endoscopic examination, which revealed erosive disease. Melanie has made a serious medication error by administering warfarin to the patient, who is recovering post-operatively.

SIMULATION LEARNING OBJECTIVES

1. Employ strategies to reduce risk of harm to the patient.

2. Perform priority nursing actions based on assessment and clinical data.

3. Reassess/monitor patient status following nursing interventions.

4. Communicate appropriately with other healthcare team members in a timely, organized, patient-specific manner.

5. Make clinical judgments and decisions that are evidence-based.

6. Practice within nursing scope of practice.

7. Demonstrate knowledge of legal and ethical obligations.

SIMULATION SCENARIO OBJECTIVES

1. Reflect on actions taken by self and peers as a medically adverse event unfolds.

2. Demonstrate trauma-informed communication techniques to support the provider who has made the error.

3. Deconstruct the error from an individual and systems approach with recommendations to prevent similar errors from occurring in the future.

PRIOR TO THE SIMULATION, THE STUDENT SHOULD:

WATCH THE VIDEO:

- Johns Hopkins Medicine. (2015). *The RISE program: Peer support for caregivers in distress.* Retrieved from https://www.youtube.com/watch?v=NiLEWpjNP6I

READ:

Delacroix, R. (2017). Exploring the experience of nurse practitioners who have committed medical errors: A phenomenological approach. *Journal of the American Association of Nurse Practitioners, 29,* 403–409. doi: 10.1002/2327-6924.12468

Scott, S. D., Hirschinger, L. E., Cox, K. R., McCoig, M., Hahn-Cover, K., Epperly, K. M., . . . Hall, L. W. (2010). Caring for our own: Deploying a systemwide second victim rapid response team. *The Joint Commission Journal on Quality and Patient Safety, 36*(5), 233–240.

Wu, A. W. (2000). The second victim: The doctor who makes the mistake needs help too. *BMJ, 320*(7237), 726–727.

PREBRIEFING/BRIEFING

The objectives of this simulation are to learn about second-victim trauma, which is experienced after a medical error, and discover ways to provide support to those making the error within a trauma-informed framework.

Simulation Design Template (revised March 2018) © 2018, National League for Nursing. Originally adapted from Childs, Sepples, & Chambers (2007), Designing simulations for nursing education. In P. R. Jeffries (Ed.), *Simulation in nursing education: From conceptualization to evaluation* (pp. 42–58). Washington, DC: National League for Nursing.

Link to original template: https://sirc.nln.org/pluginfile.php/18733/mod_page/content/51/Simulation%20Design%20Template%202018.docx

SECONDARY TRAUMA WITH POSTTRAUMATIC STRESS SYMPTOMS: UNEXPECTED PATIENT DEATH

Samuel ("Sam") is a junior nursing student preparing to graduate next year. He is in his obstetric (OB) clinical rotation and is assigned to the Wright family: mom, Tracy, and dad, Tom. Tracy is a 41-week laboring primigravida. Her difficult labor lasts 39 hours and involves considerable bleeding and a third-degree episiotomy after the baby has passed through the birth canal. After a healthy infant girl is born, Tracy begins to lose an estimated 900 mL more blood. She is transferred to the intensive care unit for blood transfusions and monitoring. Sam is unable to accompany Tracy and stays with the newborn. Unfortunately, Sam learns from his clinical instructor, Dr. Schaffer, that Tracy passed due to postpartum hemorrhage.

SIMULATION LEARNING OBJECTIVES

1. Employ strategies to reduce the risk of harm to peers.

2. Communicate with peers and the clinical instructor in a manner that illustrates caring, reflects cultural awareness, and addresses psychosocial needs.

3. Demonstrate knowledge of legal and ethical obligations.

SIMULATION SCENARIO OBJECTIVES

1. Identify the psychological reactions to secondary trauma.

2. Apply the Three E's of trauma as outlined by SAMHSA (2014)—Event, Experience, Effects—to Sam's experience.

3. List two ways to integrate self-care into professional nursing practice.

PRIOR TO THE SIMULATION, THE STUDENT SHOULD:

WATCH THE VIDEO:

- Bormann, J. (2018). *Mantram, Session 1: What Mantram is and how to choose one.* PsychArmor Institute. Retrieved from https://www.youtube.com/watch?v=tyFRGpLJ9-4&index=3&list=PL5uXbOV BSV4X6xpPz79et7GcjdoMtioYx

Note that there are four sessions to this series.

READ:

Garcia-Dia, M. J., DiNapoli, J. M., Garcia-Ona, L., Jakubowski, R., & O'Flaherty, D. (2013). Concept analysis: Resilience. *Archives of Psychiatric Nursing, 27,* 264–270. doi: http://dx.doi.org/10.1016/j.apnu.2013.07.003

Michalec, B., Diefenbeck, C., & Mahoney, M. (2013). The calm before the storm? Burnout and compassion fatigue among undergraduate nursing students. *Nurse Education Today, 33,* 314–320. doi: http://dx.doi.org/10.1016/j.nedt.2013.01.026

Niitsu, K., Houfek, J. F., Barron, C. R., Stoltengerg, S. F., Kupzyk, K. A., & Rice, M. J. (2017). A concept analysis of resilience integrating genetics. *Issues in Mental Health Nursing, 38*(11), 896–906. doi: 10.1080/01612840.2017.1350225

Substance Abuse and Mental Health Services Administration. (2014). *SAMHSA's concept of trauma and guidance for a trauma-informed approach.* HHS Publication No. (SMA) 14-4884. Rockville, MD: Author.

PERFORM SELF-ASSESSMENT: SECONDARY TRAUMATIC STRESS SCALE

See Table 3.2 (pages 73–74) in *The Influence of Psychological Trauma in Nursing.*

Bride, B. E., Robinson, M. M., & Yegidis, B. (2004). Development and validation of the Secondary Traumatic Stress Scale. *Research on Social Work Practice, 14*(1), 27–35. doi: 10.1177/1049731503254106

PREBRIEFING/BRIEFING

The objectives of this simulation are to recognize the symptoms of PTSD in self and peers after witnessing others' trauma and to identify ways to mitigate secondary traumatic stress.

Simulation Design Template (revised March 2018) © 2018, National League for Nursing. Originally adapted from Childs, Sepples, & Chambers (2007), Designing simulations for nursing education. In P. R. Jeffries (Ed.), *Simulation in nursing education: From conceptualization to evaluation* (pp. 42–58). Washington, DC: National League for Nursing.

Link to original template: https://sirc.nln.org/pluginfile.php/18733/mod_page/content/51/ Simulation%20Design%20Template%2 2018.docx

SECTION 3

TRAUMA AFTER GRADUATION: BUILDING A RESILIENT NURSING WORKFORCE

SYSTEM-INDUCED TRAUMA

Rebecca is a 62-year-old elementary schoolteacher who had been experiencing ventricular tachycardia with brief periods (seconds) of unease and dizziness. She was admitted for cardiac ablation and transferred to ICU at one day post-cardiac ablation for uncontrolled bleeding from the femoral artery post-surgical procedure. Her bleeding stabilized after a blood transfusion, and she is due to be discharged tomorrow. There is currently no bleeding from the femoral catheter incision site, and there are no signs of infection. Rebecca is adamant about "never going through something like that again!" She is asking to be discharged "ASAP!" because the hospital is a "deathtrap" and, more than likely, she'll "get some superbug that eats through my flesh." She is refusing morning care and respiratory therapy. (She is in early-stage congestive heart failure with a BMI of 31.) She also refuses to walk in the hallway and demands to know, prior to taking any medication, what its purpose is and why the physician prescribed it for her. Her husband sits in the room, silent.

SIMULATION LEARNING OBJECTIVES

1. Employ strategies to reduce the risk of further harm to the patient.

2. Conduct assessments appropriate for patient care in an organized and systematic manner.

3. Perform priority nursing actions based on assessment and clinical data.

4. Reassess/monitor the patient status following nursing interventions.

5. Communicate with the patient and the family in a manner that illustrates caring, reflects cultural awareness, and addresses psychosocial needs.

6. Communicate appropriately with other healthcare team members in a timely, organized, patient-specific manner.

7. Make clinical judgments and decisions that are evidence-based.

8. Practice within nursing scope of practice.

9. Demonstrate knowledge of legal and ethical obligations.

SIMULATION SCENARIO OBJECTIVES

1. Recognize the signs and symptoms of medical trauma experienced by those who have been treated in ICU, which could lead to unfair labeling of patient behaviors.

2. Design interventions that mitigate PTSS experienced by patients post-ICU.

3. Within a traumatic stress framework, use therapeutic communication techniques to raise patient awareness of their experiences.

PRIOR TO THE SIMULATION, THE STUDENT SHOULD:

WATCH THE VIDEO:

- Johns Hopkins Medicine. (2014). *ICU diaries help prevent PTSD: JHM piloting the initiative.* Retrieved from https://www.youtube.com/watch?v=abMPULXpUVw

READ:

Marsac, M. L., Kassam-Adams, N., Delahanty, D. L., Widaman, K. F., & Barakat, L. P. (2014). Posttraumatic stress following medical trauma in children: A proposed model of bio-psycho-social processes during the peri-trauma period. *Clinical Child and Family Psychological Review, 17,* 399–411. doi: 10.1007/s10567-014-0174-2

Walz, G. R., & Bleuer, J. C. (2013). When treatment becomes trauma: Defining, preventing, and transforming medical trauma. *VISTAS Online,* Article 73. Retrieved from https://www.counseling.org/docs/default-source/vistas/when-treatment-becomes-trauma-defining-preventing-.pdf

PREBRIEFING/BRIEFING

The objective of this simulation is to learn about system-induced or medical trauma. This type of trauma is experienced due to care rendered and as the aftereffects of such care are realized. Interpreting patient behaviors within this context is the focus of this activity.

Simulation Design Template (revised March 2018) © 2018, National League for Nursing. Originally adapted from Childs, Sepples, & Chambers (2007), Designing simulations for nursing education. In P. R. Jeffries (Ed.), *Simulation in nursing education: From conceptualization to evaluation* (pp. 42–58). Washington, DC: National League for Nursing.

Link to original template: https://sirc.nln.org/pluginfile.php/18733/mod_page/content/51/Simulation%20Design%20Template%202018.docx

WORKPLACE VIOLENCE

An emergency department (ED) nurse, Lizzie, was seriously injured by a patient on ecstasy. As a result of the attack, Lizzie suffered a concussion, broken jaw, and two broken ribs. After eight weeks, she has been released to resume employment but is struggling in her performance. Her coworkers have been complaining to the ED manager, Carol, that Lizzie has been "slacking" and unengaged with patients, forcing other nurses to cover for her, and frequently calling off.

SIMULATION LEARNING OBJECTIVES

1. Employ strategies to reduce risk of harm to the nurse.

2. Conduct assessments appropriate for nursing care in an organized and systematic manner.

3. Perform priority nursing actions based on assessment and clinical data.

4. Reassess/monitor nurse status following interventions.

5. Communicate with the nurse in a manner that illustrates caring, reflects cultural awareness, and addresses psychosocial needs.

6. Communicate appropriately with other healthcare team members in a timely, organized, patient-specific manner.

7. Make supervisory and clinical judgments and decisions that are evidence-based.

8. Demonstrate knowledge of legal and ethical obligations.

SIMULATION SCENARIO OBJECTIVES

1. Design a therapeutic discussion between a nurse who has experienced workplace violence and a trauma-informed supervisor.

2. Substitute nontherapeutic dialogue with appropriate dialogue when counseling a nurse who has experienced trauma related to workplace violence.

3. Build strategies to support personal safety when rendering care to patients and their families.

PRIOR TO THE SIMULATION, THE STUDENT SHOULD:

READ:

National Child Traumatic Stress Network. (2018). *Using the secondary traumatic stress core competencies in trauma-informed supervision.* Retrieved from https://www.nctsn.org/sites/default/files/resources/fact-sheet/using_the_secondary_traumatic_stress_core_competencies_in_trauma-informed_supervision.pdf

Speroni, K. G., Fitch, T., Dawson, E., Dugan, L., & Atherton, M. (2014). Incidence and cost of nurse workplace violence perpetrated by hospital patients or patient visitors. *Journal of Emergency Nursing, 40*(3), 218–228. doi: https://doi.org/10.1016/j.jen.2013.05.014

Wei, C-Y., Chiou, S-T., Chien, L-Y., & Huang, N. (2016). Workplace violence against nurses—Prevalence and association with hospital organizational characteristics and health-promotion efforts: Cross-sectional study. *International Journal of Nursing Studies, 56*, 63–70. doi: http://dx.doi.org/10.1016/j.ijnurstu.2015.12.012

Zhang, L., Wang, A., Xiec, X., Zhouc, Y., Lid, J., Yange, L., & Zhang, J. (2017). Workplace violence against nurses: A cross-sectional study. *International Journal of Nursing Studies, 72*, 8–14. doi: https://doi.org/10.1016/jinurstu.2017.04.002

ENROLL IN COURSE ON WORKPLACE VIOLENCE:

National Institute for Occupational Safety and Health: Centers for Disease Control and Prevention. (2016). Workplace violence prevention for nurses. Retrieved from https://wwwn.cdc.gov/wpvhc/Course.aspx/Slide/Intro_2

PREBRIEFING/BRIEFING

The objective of this simulation is to learn about the posttraumatic stress symptoms following workplace violence/injury. The simulation also brings forth an appreciation of a trauma-informed nursing supervisor and the support offered to employees who have experienced a traumatic event.

Simulation Design Template (revised March 2018) © 2018, National League for Nursing. Originally adapted from Childs, Sepples, & Chambers (2007), Designing simulations for nursing education. In P. R. Jeffries (Ed.), *Simulation in nursing education: From conceptualization to evaluation* (pp. 42–58). Washington, DC: National League for Nursing.

Link to original template: https://sirc.nln.org/pluginfile.php/18733/mod_page/content/51/Simulation%20Design%20Template%202018.docx

ENDING THOUGHTS ON TRAUMA SIMULATIONS

We hope you've identified an important theme: The nurse as a person and professional needs care and compassion post trauma. We often don't extend this care to self, nor see nurses as recipients of care, but this needs to change. There are multiple opportunities to provide significant support for one another at the right time in the right place. We need to extend our talents to our fellow nurses, especially with our professional world being so crowded with trauma. Although these simulations don't depend on technology as many activities do, they present opportunities to learn and practice critical skills—and as importantly—prepare for situations that involve different forms of trauma our patients and peers are exposed to.

POSTTRAUMATIC GROWTH

We want to stress that posttraumatic growth and resiliency can also result from trauma. Obviously, it's not a matter of whether you will be confronted with trauma directly or indirectly (secondary trauma); it is a matter of when and how frequently. As such, remember that through the process of trauma recovery, there may be internal growth, as well as increased resiliency and inner strength. We believe this will translate to more compassionate, attuned care for yourself, your peers, and your vulnerable patients.